Internal Dialogue

Lavanya Talati

BookLeaf
Publishing

India | USA | UK

Dedication

this book is dedicated to my mother, Radhika
you're pure magic

Preface

This is a collection of 21 poems pulled from different phases of my life. They are a space in time each, capturing human fears, aches and insecurities, with a thread of spiritual breakthroughs weaved through them.

My hope is you will find comfort and camaraderie in these poems. That you will come to believe that - even in your darkest feelings and thoughts, you are not alone. We all build these internal worlds with conversations no one else will hear, building narrative upon narrative, essentially writing a long novel that becomes our lives.

You are getting a glimpse into mine; this is my internal dialogue.

While a lot of these poems deal with insecurity, heartbreak and pain, they also speak of renewal and hope. Our lives are still being written, so let's ensure we write stories that make our souls fill with joy and resilience.

i love you, read leisurely.

Acknowledgements

Thank you to the universe allowing me to interact with poetry and songs in this life. Not a single poem is written by just the writer, it is always through play with the divine.

I want to thank my dear family & friends for loving me and being a rock solid foundation. It is because of you that I have the space and support to write and be vulnerable.

Lastly, thank you to bookleaf publishing for catering to young unheard writers and giving us a platform.

old tree

there's an old tree
outside my balcony
she was there before;
will remain after me
every October
she sheds her leaves
by summer
the flowers fly down to me

sometimes i look out
with jealousy
how does she lose
everything she builds?
how does she grow
everything that leaves?
if I stare long enough
maybe she'll teach me her tricks
if I stay still like her,
maybe the cycle will begin

circus act

I know the girls you talk about;
you loved before
the last one played puppeteer,
but you called her yours

how much more can I take
just to hold you close?
you call her your ex,
but you don't label anymore

so I pretend
cause I'm down so bad
and you pretend
that you don't understand

truth is it hurts you hurting me
but we're both selfish
so we don't leave

A circus act for empty seats

mom always says:

everything you lose
 is meant to go

everywhere you've been
 has made you so

there's light in everything
 if you just look

and stop to feel the wind
 over your soul

the love, it -

you lived in this space once
206 bones and flesh holding you up
breathing, talking, filling cups
holding my hand, weaving a world
you've gone away, but you're here
swirled into my choices, my eyes, all my years
in the way I like to love, in poetry and phrases
you raised me for this day, now I'm here, facing it
I'm mad and sad and I miss you like a little kid
if I close my eyes, I can feel you, like the morning wind

the love, it never leaves

ego speaking

am I really as forgettable as I think?
old ink spilt on paper always sinks
do you never think about me babe?
not even when you're drunk on another date?

am I really as childlike as I seem?
toys get old as age changes things
have you discarded me to the side of your playroom?
leave me when she brings a doll brand new?

am I really as small as I imagine?
thoughts growing bigger than an elephant
i try to hide under tables and inside bathrooms
if I let it out will it fill this vacuum?

am i really as naive as you say?
a clueless wanderer that becomes the prey
a young bride that knows she wed too soon
no home feels familiar by the day

am i really as beautiful in your eyes?
dancing like a flower, bathing in sunlight

beauty never really made anybody stay
for everything appealing the end awaits

being

warm green tea or cold coffee
slipping into a routine at home
watching trees & playing with animals
loving the people around me till I overdose
trips twice a year to somewhere new
doing the thing i'm not quite ready to do
deep conversations about the wonders of life
people that care and love to thrive
moving my body to the sound of my breath
loving someone with reckless care
writing about my forages of life
someone to listen to the words I conspire
horses and fields of endless grass
mountains and beaches to quench my heart
watching the sun rise on a random day
the smile of someone who's lost and loved anyway
whispers of the hearts that let me in
a quiet mind settling in
some things that bring meaning to being

lesson

it's half past 11
10 beers 4 candles
crying in your bathroom

thinking to myself

maybe i should stop this now
sail back to my home town
your world isn't for me so
I'll pack my things and go

it 's tuesday the 10th
4 friends 11 texts
pacing in my room

all I think about is you

and the doors you choose
how they cut me loose
you never fought for me so
I taught myself how to lock my door

you're a lesson I want to let go of

two whole truths

they say
a writer needs pain
like a jet ski
needs fuel

every so often
I fear
if I let go
I wont be any good

if I had to choose
between
happiness or a rhyme
I wonder what i'd do

I refuse to believe
they must be the same
the craft & the pain
are 2 whole truths

faith works where you put it
what hurts is not the only fuel -
I refuse, I refuse, I refuse

chinese whisperer

you come to me
distraught
with eyes full of
regret
heavy pockets &
a heavy heart
in a small,
faraway voice
you take back
what you said
telling me
you didn't mean it
you're lost
in the layers
of self hate
you never know
what you want to say
you're a
chinese whisperer
by the day

mirror

they say the mirror never lies
so I ask "who's looking?"

one reflection
has infinite truths
and a slew of dishonest happenings

am I honest
when I pick at my skin?
my colour, my weight, the words of my kin

am I honest
when I see beauty in my eyes?
a shade of brown no one thinks is inspiring

they say the mirror never lies
so I ask, "who's looking?"

-- when do we see the truth?

waves of sorrow

the waves of sorrow
have taken over me
I fall over tides
I used to surf on

something's amiss
its not my day
and the feeling in my chest
gets harder to ignore

so I try to rest
read a book or
watch the sunset
but my mind keeps chattering on

what do I do?
on days like these
where do I go
to keep my head above ground

one

I close my eyes
I block it all out
I am the universe
I am nobody ..

traversing through
an infinite illusion
there are times like these
where I awake -
suddenly

to a voice inside of me
one that never sleeps
past the veil of my egoic ways
telling me with certainty

"you're everything
you're nothing
you're whole
you're part of a sum

open your eyes
realize

you & the world,
have always been one"

internal dialogue

you're the words I write but never show
the coffee that's too far to drive for
the dreams I think but never grow
the arms that held me but let me go

the trains I missed while going home
the stories that were never told
the seeds I water but never grow
the arms that held me but let me go

circling my mind
just skating on
i'd join you in the ring
but you're so beautiful
just out of my reach
baby, carry on

empty house

have you ever been here?
four walls laden with all your fears
careful steps in the dark
falling face down over cracks

hands trembling for any support
silent screams that no one knows
how could they when you never spoke
should've told someone when you locked the door

shaking your head in the shallows now
shaky breaths on hollow ground
make a tiny fist and stand up now
muster the courage to rise when you fall

pull the curtains back,
you never needed a switch
just a brutal reminder
of the light that exists

open your eyes to summer rays
let go of the comfort of sad days
pack your things and move away
you don't have to stay in an empty house

something familiar

amid air I smelt
something familiar
the way it was a kiss
breaking my demeanor
a long lost bliss
I scramble to remember
the feel, the scent
of your voice in my ear

amid air I smelt
something familiar
the way you lost your cool
breaking your demeanor
a pain that stings
every other winter
the silent death
of heartbreak in my ear

coffee

my day old coffee
sits in the sink
I've been too occupied
by my thoughts
to wash the dishes clean

brown liquid
loosing its color
curdling on itself
losing its flavor
we feel familiar
to each other

love is drama

I'd trade every sunset hour
to hold your hand under a black sky

I'd love every loveless town
if it meant we could see dawn
after the night

I'd marry you the first time you ask me
but darling, you never offer

I lie by your side with eyes-wide wonder
yet all you do is sigh

I die slowly, cutting my loses
knowing the thorn in your side

for you, love is drama
and I, your playwright

slighted

I feel slighted
like you don't care

like I'll bury this feeling
deep inside my chest

to keep you in the face of
losing myself

tremor

looking into your eyes
I feel a tremor down my spine
I said never again
but here I am -
no parachutes by my side

I take the risk of falling
to feel the wind,

your hand in mine

take a breath

relax your shoulders
take a breath in
breathe a breath out

the birds will still sing
the world will still spin
life will go on

you're not really alone
it's just a green screen
of your thoughts

something real

it's so stupid
how good this feels
you're sleeping with your limbs
wrapped around me

I watch you breathe
I burn it in my mind
I hear you dream
now I can hear my own voice

it pours out of you
and onto our bed
I'm overwhelmed,
 im so scared

to be in something real

this is oh so real